I0012593

Secure Remote Work: Protecting Your Workforce in the Digital Age

A Practical Guide to Safeguarding Your Business, Data, and Employees from Cyber Threats in a Remote Environment

By

Mark David

© **[Mark David].**
All rights reserved.

This handbook is protected by copyright law. No part of this publication may be reproduced, distributed, or transmitted in any form or by any means, including photocopying, recording, or other electronic or mechanical methods, without the prior written permission of the author.

Table of contents

Introduction: The Shift to Remote Work

The Evolution of Work: From Office to Home

The concept of work has undergone a radical transformation in the last few decades. Historically, work was synonymous with physical office spaces, where employees gathered daily to collaborate, complete tasks, and contribute to organizational goals. This centralized model offered organizations a sense of control, as employees worked within a controlled environment with robust security measures. However, the advent of technology has fundamentally disrupted this paradigm.

The rise of the internet, cloud computing, and digital communication tools has made remote work not only possible but increasingly preferred. Initially adopted as a perk to attract talent or as a necessity for freelancers, remote work gained massive traction during the COVID-19 pandemic. Lockdowns and social distancing forced businesses to embrace remote work overnight, proving that many roles could be effectively performed outside traditional office settings. Today, remote and hybrid work models are no longer seen as temporary solutions but as integral parts of modern business operations.

Key Factors Driving the Shift:

1. **Technological Advancements**: Cloud services, collaboration tools like Slack and Microsoft Teams, and virtual private networks (VPNs) have enabled employees to work from virtually anywhere.
2. **Global Talent Pool**: Organizations can now hire talent regardless of geographical boundaries, fostering diversity and reducing recruitment limitations.
3. **Cost-Effectiveness**: Remote work significantly reduces

overhead costs for businesses by minimizing expenses related to office space, utilities, and on-site infrastructure.

4. **Work-Life Balance**: Many employees prefer remote work for its flexibility, which allows them to balance personal and professional commitments more effectively.

Despite its advantages, the shift to remote work has introduced new vulnerabilities that businesses must address proactively.

Cybersecurity Challenges in Remote Work Environments

As businesses embrace remote work, they inadvertently expand their digital footprint, creating new entry points for cybercriminals. Unlike centralized office environments where security measures are easier to implement and monitor, remote work environments are inherently decentralized. This decentralization poses unique cybersecurity challenges.

Key Challenges:

1. **Insecure Home Networks**: Many employees work from home on networks that lack the robust security features of corporate environments. Default passwords, outdated routers, and unencrypted networks are common vulnerabilities.

2. **Device Security Risks**: Remote employees often use personal devices to access work systems. These devices may lack adequate security software, making them susceptible to malware, ransomware, and phishing attacks.

3. **Data Breaches and Unauthorized Access**:

With sensitive business data being accessed from various locations, the risk of unauthorized access increases. A lost or stolen device, for instance, can lead to a major data breach.

4. **Phishing and Social Engineering Attacks**:
   Remote workers are prime targets for phishing scams, as they may lack immediate access to IT support for verifying suspicious emails or links.

5. **Unsecured Collaboration Tools**:
   The widespread use of video conferencing, messaging apps, and file-sharing platforms can expose sensitive information if these tools are not properly secured.

6. **Compliance Challenges**:
   Remote work complicates

compliance with data protection regulations like GDPR, HIPAA, and CCPA. Ensuring that employees adhere to these standards while working remotely requires additional oversight.

The Rising Threat Landscape

Cybercriminals have capitalized on the vulnerabilities of remote work, launching targeted attacks against individuals and organizations. A report by cybersecurity firms indicates a sharp rise in phishing attempts and ransomware attacks aimed at remote workers since the pandemic. Without proactive measures, these threats can result in financial losses, reputational damage, and legal liabilities.

Why Securing Remote Work is Critical for Businesses

The importance of securing remote work cannot be overstated. For businesses, the stakes are incredibly high, with consequences that go far beyond financial losses.

1. Protecting Sensitive Data

Remote work often involves the handling of sensitive customer data, proprietary business information, and intellectual property. A single breach can lead to severe consequences, including loss of customer trust and potential lawsuits.

2. Ensuring Business Continuity

Cyberattacks can disrupt business operations, resulting in downtime and lost productivity. In a remote work setting, this disruption can spread quickly, affecting the entire workforce and halting critical processes.

3. Maintaining Regulatory Compliance

Failure to secure remote work environments can lead to non-compliance with data protection laws. Regulatory penalties can be steep, adding another layer of risk for businesses.

4. Preserving Reputation

Customers and stakeholders expect businesses to safeguard their data. A cybersecurity incident can damage a company's reputation, leading to a loss of business and customer confidence.

5. Adapting to Future Trends

The remote work trend is here to stay. Businesses that fail to adapt and implement robust security measures will struggle to compete in an increasingly digital and decentralized world.

Conclusion

The shift to remote work represents a paradigm change in how businesses operate. While it offers flexibility and cost savings, it also introduces significant cybersecurity challenges. For businesses to thrive in this new environment, they must prioritize securing their remote work infrastructure, educating employees on cybersecurity best practices, and leveraging advanced security tools. In doing so, they can unlock the full potential of remote work while safeguarding their operations against evolving cyber threats.

Chapter 1: Understanding Cyber Threats in Remote Work

The adoption of remote work has opened new opportunities for businesses, but it has also exposed them to a growing array of cybersecurity threats. Cybercriminals are exploiting the vulnerabilities inherent in decentralized work environments, targeting employees and organizational systems with increasingly sophisticated attacks. Understanding these threats is the first step toward building a resilient remote work security strategy.

Common Threats Targeting Remote Workers

Remote workers face unique cybersecurity challenges due to their reliance on personal devices, home networks, and remote access to organizational systems. Below are the most prevalent threats targeting remote work environments:

1. Phishing Attacks and Social Engineering

Phishing is one of the most common and effective methods cybercriminals use to gain unauthorized access to sensitive information. In a phishing attack, attackers send deceptive emails, messages, or phone calls designed to trick employees into revealing credentials, downloading malicious files, or clicking on malicious links.

Key Characteristics of Phishing Attacks:

- Emails impersonating trusted entities such as banks, government agencies, or even the employee's organization.
- Messages that create urgency, such as "Your account will be deactivated in 24 hours unless you act."

- Links leading to fake websites designed to steal login credentials.

Social Engineering Tactics:
Social engineering exploits human psychology rather than technical vulnerabilities. Common tactics include:

- **Pretexting**: Creating a fabricated scenario to manipulate the target into providing information.
- **Baiting**: Offering something enticing, such as free downloads, to lure victims into exposing sensitive data.
- **Tailgating**: Gaining physical access to a secure area by tricking someone into granting entry.

Impact on Remote Workers:

- Compromised credentials can lead to unauthorized access to corporate networks.

- Sensitive data, including customer information and trade secrets, can be stolen or leaked.

2. Ransomware and Malware Infections

Ransomware attacks involve encrypting an organization's data and demanding payment to restore access. Malware, on the other hand, refers to malicious software designed to damage systems, steal data, or spy on users.

How Ransomware and Malware Spread:

- Through phishing emails with malicious attachments or links.
- Via unsecure downloads from non-reputable websites.
- Through outdated software and operating systems vulnerable to exploitation.

Consequences for Remote Work Environments:

- Loss of access to critical systems and data.
- Significant financial losses, including ransom payments and recovery costs.
- Reputational damage and loss of customer trust.

3. Insider Threats and Human Error

Not all threats come from external attackers. Insider threats and human error play a significant role in compromising cybersecurity.

Insider Threats:

- Malicious insiders: Employees or contractors who intentionally misuse their access to harm the organization.

- Negligent insiders: Employees who inadvertently expose systems to risk, such as by sharing passwords or mishandling sensitive data.

Human Error:

- Sending sensitive information to the wrong recipient.
- Falling victim to phishing scams.
- Using weak or reused passwords across multiple accounts.

Mitigation Strategies:

- Regular training to educate employees about cybersecurity risks.
- Implementing strict access controls and monitoring user activity.

Real-World Examples of Remote Work Cyber Incidents

Example 1: The Colonial Pipeline Ransomware Attack (2021)

A remote work credential was compromised, leading to a ransomware attack that shut down the pipeline's operations. The attackers demanded a ransom of $4.4 million, highlighting the dangers of weak access controls.

Example 2: Zoom Bombing Incidents (2020)

As businesses shifted to video conferencing during the pandemic, unsecured Zoom meetings were hijacked by attackers, exposing sensitive discussions and confidential information.

Example 3: Twitter Insider Attack (2020)

An insider threat led to the compromise of high-profile Twitter accounts, including those of Elon Musk and Barack Obama. The attackers exploited remote work policies to gain unauthorized access.

Identifying Vulnerabilities in a Remote Work Setup

To effectively combat cyber threats, organizations must identify and address vulnerabilities in their remote work environments. Key areas of concern include:

1. **Weak Authentication Mechanisms**:

    o Lack of multi-factor authentication (MFA) increases the risk of unauthorized access.
2. **Unsecured Devices and Networks**:

- Personal devices and home Wi-Fi networks often lack enterprise-grade security measures.

3. **Improper Data Storage and Sharing Practices**:

   - Employees may store sensitive data on personal devices or share files through unsecured platforms.

4. **Inadequate Monitoring and Logging**:

   - Without proper monitoring, organizations may fail to detect and respond to cyber incidents promptly.

5. **Lack of Employee Training**:

   - Employees unaware of cybersecurity best practices are more likely to fall victim to attacks.

FAQs: Common Questions About Cyber Threats

Q1: How can remote workers recognize phishing emails?

A: Look for red flags such as unfamiliar senders, urgent requests, suspicious links, and poor grammar. Always verify emails by contacting the sender directly through official channels.

Q2: What steps should I take if I suspect a ransomware infection?

A: Disconnect the infected device from the network, inform your IT department, and avoid paying the ransom. Use backup data to restore systems if available.

Q3: Are personal devices safe to use for remote work?

A: Personal devices can be safe if secured with strong passwords, updated software, and reliable antivirus programs. However, organizations should enforce a bring-your-own-device

(BYOD) policy with clear security guidelines.

Q4: How can organizations mitigate insider threats?

A: Implement strict access controls, monitor employee activities, conduct background checks, and provide cybersecurity awareness training.

Q5: What tools can enhance remote work security?

A: Use tools such as VPNs, endpoint protection software, password managers, and secure file-sharing platforms to reduce risks.

This chapter provides a detailed overview of the cybersecurity threats remote workers face and actionable insights to mitigate these risks. By addressing common vulnerabilities, organizations can build a more secure and resilient remote work environment.

Chapter 2: Securing Home Networks

Securing home networks is a fundamental aspect of protecting remote work environments from cyber threats. Unlike corporate offices equipped with robust IT infrastructure, home networks are often vulnerable due to weaker security protocols, default settings, and a lack of regular monitoring. This chapter provides a comprehensive guide to securing home networks, ensuring a safer online workspace.

Setting Up a Secure Home Wi-Fi Network

The Wi-Fi network serves as the backbone of any remote work environment. An unsecured or poorly configured Wi-Fi network can be an open invitation for cybercriminals. Strengthening the security of your Wi-Fi is the first step toward a safe digital workspace.

Default Passwords: A Security Risk

Most routers and modems come with default usernames and passwords. Cybercriminals can easily find these defaults online, making it imperative to change them immediately. Use a strong, unique password for both the router login and the Wi-Fi network.

How to Change Your Router Password:

1. Log in to your router's settings by typing its IP address (e.g., 192.168.1.1) into a web browser.
2. Use the default login credentials to access the admin panel.
3. Navigate to the settings section to update the router password.

Enable WPA3 Encryption

Wi-Fi Protected Access (WPA) is the

standard for securing wireless networks. WPA3, the latest encryption protocol, provides enhanced security by:

- Protecting against brute-force attacks.
- Offering forward secrecy to secure data even if encryption keys are compromised.
- Encrypting data individually for better privacy.

Ensure your router is set to WPA3. If it doesn't support WPA3, use WPA2 but consider upgrading your router.

Avoiding Public Wi-Fi and Safe Alternatives

Risks of Public Wi-Fi
Public Wi-Fi networks, such as those in cafes or airports, are inherently insecure. Attackers can intercept unencrypted traffic or set up fake Wi-Fi hotspots to steal sensitive information.

Safe Alternatives:

1. **Mobile Hotspots**: Use your smartphone's hotspot feature to create a private, secure internet connection.
2. **Virtual Private Networks (VPNs)**: A VPN encrypts your internet traffic, protecting it from eavesdroppers. Choose a reputable VPN provider with strong encryption protocols.
3. **Secure Wi-Fi Tethering**: Tethering your computer to your mobile device using a USB cable is another secure option.

Firewalls and Network Segmentation for Home Offices

Firewalls and network segmentation are critical components of a secure home network, especially for those who handle sensitive or confidential work.

Firewalls: Your First Line of Defense

A firewall acts as a barrier between your network and potential external threats. It monitors incoming and outgoing traffic, blocking malicious activity.

Steps to Enable and Optimize Firewalls:

1. Ensure the built-in firewall on your router is enabled.
2. Use software firewalls on all connected devices. Most operating systems, such as Windows and macOS, include built-in firewalls.
3. Configure the firewall to block suspicious IP addresses and restrict unnecessary traffic.

Network Segmentation for Enhanced Security

Network segmentation involves dividing your home network into separate segments to limit the spread of potential breaches.

Why Segment Your Network?

1. **Isolation of IoT Devices**: Internet of Things (IoT) devices are often less secure. Placing them on a separate network reduces their access to sensitive data.
2. **Work and Personal Separation**: Creating distinct networks for work and personal activities minimizes the risk of work-related data being compromised.

How to Segment Your Network:

- Use your router's guest network feature for IoT devices or personal use.
- Set up VLANs (Virtual Local Area Networks) if your router supports them.
- Assign unique passwords to each network segment.

Ensuring IoT Device Security

IoT devices, such as smart thermostats, security cameras, and voice assistants, are convenient but often vulnerable to cyberattacks. Securing these devices is essential to maintaining a safe home network.

Key IoT Security Practices

1. **Change Default Credentials**: Similar to routers, IoT devices come with default usernames and passwords. Always update these to strong, unique passwords.

2. **Regular Firmware Updates**: Manufacturers frequently release updates to patch security vulnerabilities. Enable automatic updates whenever possible.

3. **Disable Unnecessary Features**: Turn off features like

remote access or Universal Plug
and Play (UPnP) unless absolutely
necessary.

4. **Monitor Device Activity**: Use
   network monitoring tools to detect
   unusual activity from IoT devices.

5. **Connect IoT Devices to a
   Separate Network**: Isolating
   IoT devices limits their ability to
   compromise critical systems if
   they are hacked.

FAQs: Securing Internet Connections

**Q1: How can I tell if my Wi-Fi network is
secure?**
 A: Check your router settings to ensure
you're using WPA3 or WPA2 encryption.
Additionally, verify that the router's
admin password has been changed from
the default.

Q2: What is the best password practice for Wi-Fi?

A: Use a strong, unique password with a mix of uppercase letters, lowercase letters, numbers, and special characters. Avoid common phrases or easily guessable information.

Q3: Are all VPNs safe for remote work?

A: Not all VPNs are reliable. Avoid free VPNs, as they often lack robust security features. Opt for paid, reputable services like NordVPN, ExpressVPN, or CyberGhost.

Q4: What should I do if my router's firmware is outdated?

A: Check the manufacturer's website for firmware updates. Follow the instructions to download and install the latest version.

Q5: Can I use a single network for work and personal activities?

A: While it's possible, it's not

recommended. Segmenting your network improves security and minimizes the risk of a breach affecting both personal and work systems.

By following these practices, remote workers can significantly reduce the risk of cyberattacks and ensure their home networks are equipped to support a safe and productive work environment.

Chapter 3: Device Security for Remote Work

Remote work relies heavily on various devices, such as laptops, smartphones, and tablets. These devices, often referred to as endpoints, are gateways to sensitive corporate data. However, their portability and frequent use outside of secure office networks make them prime targets for cyberattacks. This chapter explores the importance of endpoint security, best practices for securing devices, and essential tools to fortify defenses.

Importance of Endpoint Security

Endpoints are the final line of defense between cybercriminals and sensitive information. Ensuring their security is critical to safeguarding corporate assets and maintaining productivity in a remote work environment.

The Growing Threat to Endpoints

Cybercriminals exploit endpoints to gain unauthorized access to corporate systems. Common threats include:

- **Phishing attacks:** Malicious emails trick employees into downloading malware or revealing credentials.
- **Ransomware attacks:** These can lock devices or encrypt data, demanding payment for access.
- **Unauthorized access:** Lost or stolen devices can lead to data breaches.

Given the risks, endpoint security is not optional but a necessity. Effective endpoint security minimizes vulnerabilities and mitigates potential damages.

Impact on Businesses

A single compromised device can have cascading effects, including:

1. **Data Breaches:** Sensitive customer or financial data can be leaked, resulting in financial and reputational losses.
2. **Operational Disruptions:** Malware infections can render devices unusable, halting productivity.
3. **Regulatory Penalties:** Failing to secure devices may violate data protection laws like GDPR or HIPAA.

By securing endpoints, businesses can protect not only their assets but also their employees and clients.

Best Practices for Securing Laptops, Smartphones, and Tablets

Remote workers often use multiple devices, making it essential to implement comprehensive security measures for each.

1. Securing Laptops

Laptops are the primary devices for remote work and, therefore, a major focus of endpoint security.

- **Update and Patch Regularly:** Keep operating systems (Windows, macOS, Linux) and software up to date. Enable automatic updates to ensure vulnerabilities are patched promptly.

- **Use a Strong Password or Biometric Login:** Avoid simple passwords. Instead,

create complex, unique passwords
or use biometric options like
fingerprint or facial recognition for
added security.

- **Implement Full-Disk
  Encryption:**
  Full-disk encryption ensures that
  even if a laptop is stolen, the data
  remains unreadable without the
  decryption key. Built-in tools like
  BitLocker (Windows) and
  FileVault (macOS) make this
  process seamless.

- **Enable Remote Wipe:**
  Configure remote wipe
  capabilities to erase data from lost
  or stolen laptops. Services like
  Microsoft Intune or Apple's Find
  My Mac are effective options.

2. Securing Smartphones and Tablets

Smartphones and tablets are increasingly used for remote work, but their portability makes them vulnerable to theft and unauthorized access.

- **Install Security Software:**
  Mobile security apps, such as Avast or McAfee, provide antivirus protection, phishing detection, and malware scanning.

- **Enable Two-Step Verification:**
  Use a second layer of verification (e.g., SMS or app-based) for sensitive apps, such as email and cloud storage.

- **Restrict App Permissions:**
  Limit app permissions to only what's necessary. For instance, avoid granting access to location or camera features unless

required.

- **Encrypt Communications:**
  Use encrypted messaging apps
  like Signal or WhatsApp for secure
  communications.

3. General Practices for All Devices

Regardless of the type of device, there
are universal security practices every
remote worker should follow:

- **Avoid Public Charging
  Stations:**
  Public USB ports can be tampered
  with to deploy malware (a tactic
  known as "juice jacking"). Use
  your own charger or a USB data
  blocker.

- **Disable Unused Features:**
  Turn off Bluetooth, NFC, and
  Wi-Fi when not in use to reduce

exposure to attacks.

- **Conduct Regular Backups:**
  Store backups securely in the cloud or on encrypted external drives. This ensures data recovery in case of ransomware or device failure.

Antivirus Software, Encryption, and Secure Configurations

To counteract modern cyber threats, leveraging tools like antivirus software, encryption, and secure configurations is critical.

Antivirus Software: The First Layer of Defense

Antivirus software detects and removes malware before it can cause damage. While operating systems have built-in options, third-party antivirus solutions often provide enhanced features.

Key Features to Look For:

1. **Real-Time Scanning:** Continuously monitors your device for threats.
2. **Phishing Protection:** Blocks malicious links in emails or websites.
3. **Behavioral Analysis:** Identifies suspicious behavior, even from unknown threats.

Top Antivirus Recommendations:

- Norton 360: Offers comprehensive protection with added VPN services.
- Bitdefender: Known for high malware detection rates and system efficiency.
- Kaspersky: Provides robust protection with minimal system impact.

Encryption: Safeguarding Data

Encryption converts data into unreadable code, ensuring it can't be accessed without the correct decryption key.

Types of Encryption for Remote Workers:

- **File-Level Encryption:** Encrypts specific files or folders for selective protection. Tools like AxCrypt or VeraCrypt can be used.
- **Email Encryption:** Protects sensitive communication using tools like ProtonMail or Microsoft Outlook's encryption features.

Secure Configurations: Hardening Devices

Secure configurations reduce potential attack vectors by limiting unnecessary features and enhancing device settings.

Steps to Securely Configure Devices:

1. Disable administrative privileges for daily use.
2. Use a secure DNS provider like Cloudflare or OpenDNS.
3. Configure automatic screen locks to activate after periods of inactivity.

Using Multi-Factor Authentication (MFA) for All Devices

MFA adds a critical layer of security by requiring multiple verification factors to access devices or applications.

Types of MFA:

- **SMS-Based MFA:** Sends a one-time code via text.
- **Authenticator Apps:** Generate time-sensitive codes on your smartphone (e.g., Google Authenticator, Authy).

- **Hardware Tokens:** Physical devices like YubiKey for secure access.

Why MFA is Essential:

1. **Prevents Unauthorized Access:** Even if passwords are compromised, MFA requires an additional factor to gain entry.
2. **Mitigates Phishing Attacks:** Compromised credentials alone are insufficient for attackers.

Implementing MFA for Remote Work:

1. Enable MFA for all corporate accounts and devices.
2. Use application-specific passwords for better control.
3. Regularly review MFA configurations for updates and improvements.

FAQs: Protecting Work Devices

Q1: Can antivirus software completely protect my device?

A: While antivirus software provides significant protection, no solution is foolproof. Combine it with other practices like MFA, encryption, and regular updates for comprehensive security.

Q2: How can I secure a lost or stolen device?

A: Use remote wipe tools to erase data, and ensure the device is locked with a strong password or biometric authentication.

Q3: What's the difference between device encryption and file encryption?

A: Device encryption secures the entire disk, while file encryption protects individual files or folders. Both are valuable, depending on your needs.

Q4: Should I use free antivirus software?

A: Free antivirus software offers basic protection but may lack advanced features. Paid options are more reliable for remote work.

Q5: Is public Wi-Fi safe if I use a VPN?

A: A VPN significantly enhances security on public Wi-Fi by encrypting your internet traffic, but avoid accessing sensitive accounts if possible.

By implementing these measures, remote workers can effectively secure their devices, ensuring a safe and productive digital workspace.

Chapter 4: Safe Use of Communication and Collaboration Tools

Communication and collaboration tools are the backbone of remote work. From email to messaging apps and video conferencing platforms, these tools enable seamless interaction among teams, clients, and partners. However, they are also prime targets for cybercriminals seeking to exploit vulnerabilities. This chapter delves into securing communication channels, preventing eavesdropping, safeguarding remote meetings, and implementing best practices for secure file sharing.

Securing Email, Messaging Apps, and Video Conferencing Tools

Effective cybersecurity starts with ensuring the tools you use daily are secure. Each communication tool comes with unique risks that require specific countermeasures.

1. Email Security

Email remains one of the most common communication tools and the primary vector for phishing attacks. Cybercriminals use emails to deliver malicious links, steal credentials, and spread malware.

Best Practices for Email Security:

- **Enable Multi-Factor Authentication (MFA):** Add a second layer of security to your email account.
- **Use Spam Filters:** Advanced spam filters can automatically detect and block phishing emails.
- **Verify Senders:** Always double-check the sender's address to ensure it's legitimate. Look for subtle misspellings (e.g., john@amzon.com vs. john@amazon.com).

- **Avoid Clicking on Suspicious Links:** Hover over links to view their actual destination. If in doubt, don't click.
- **Encrypt Emails:** Use end-to-end encryption tools like ProtonMail or PGP (Pretty Good Privacy) to ensure the content of your emails remains private.

2. Messaging Apps

Messaging apps like Slack, Microsoft Teams, and WhatsApp facilitate instant communication but can become entry points for unauthorized access or data leaks if not secured properly.

Best Practices for Messaging App Security:

- **Choose Encrypted Platforms:** Use apps with end-to-end encryption, such as Signal or WhatsApp.

- **Restrict Access to Workspaces:** Only allow verified users to join workspace channels.
- **Set Message Retention Policies:** Configure apps to automatically delete old messages to reduce exposure to breaches.
- **Monitor Integrations:** Limit third-party app integrations to trusted tools that align with your organization's security policies.

3. Video Conferencing Tools

Video conferencing tools like Zoom, Google Meet, and Microsoft Teams have revolutionized remote collaboration but pose unique security challenges, including unauthorized meeting access (known as "Zoombombing") and eavesdropping.

Best Practices for Video Conferencing Security:

- **Password-Protect Meetings:** Always require a password to join meetings.
- **Use Waiting Rooms:** Enable waiting rooms to vet participants before admitting them into the meeting.
- **Update Software Regularly:** Ensure the video conferencing app is updated to patch known vulnerabilities.
- **Disable Screen Sharing by Default:** Allow only the host to share their screen unless necessary.
- **Be Cautious with Meeting Links:** Avoid sharing meeting links publicly; send them directly to participants.

Preventing Eavesdropping and Data Leaks During Remote Meetings

Remote meetings often involve the discussion of sensitive information, making them attractive targets for cybercriminals. Safeguarding these interactions is crucial to maintaining business confidentiality.

1. Use Encrypted Platforms

Choose video conferencing tools that offer end-to-end encryption (E2EE). This ensures that only participants can access the conversation. Examples include:

- **Zoom with E2EE enabled:** Available for all users, ensuring meeting content is secure.
- **Microsoft Teams:** Encrypts data both in transit and at rest.

2. Authenticate Participants

Verify the identity of participants before allowing them to join. Use tools that display the participant list clearly and allow hosts to eject unauthorized users.

3. Avoid Sharing Sensitive Information Verbally or Visually

Even in secure meetings, consider the sensitivity of the information being shared. Avoid displaying confidential documents on screen and use secure file-sharing methods instead.

4. Monitor Meeting Recordings

If meetings are recorded, store the recordings securely with encryption. Restrict access to authorized personnel and delete recordings when no longer needed.

File Sharing: Best Practices for Secure Collaboration

File sharing is an essential part of remote collaboration but comes with significant risks. Unsecured file-sharing practices can lead to data breaches and malware infections.

1. Use Secure File-Sharing Platforms

Opt for platforms with built-in security features, such as Google Drive, Dropbox Business, or Microsoft OneDrive. Ensure files are encrypted during transfer and at rest.

2. Limit Access Permissions

Grant access to files on a need-to-know basis. Use role-based permissions to restrict editing, viewing, or sharing capabilities. Regularly audit access logs to identify unauthorized activities.

3. Avoid Email Attachments for Sensitive Files

Instead of emailing attachments, share files through secure cloud links. This reduces the risk of malicious file interception and allows for access control.

4. Regularly Update and Scan Shared Files

Ensure shared files are free of malware. Use antivirus tools to scan files before uploading them to collaboration platforms.

5. Encrypt Files Before Sharing

For highly sensitive files, encrypt them using tools like VeraCrypt or WinZip before sharing. Share the encryption key securely through a separate channel.

FAQs: Securing Online Communication Tools

Q1: What is the safest way to share sensitive files?
A: Use encrypted file-sharing platforms like Google Drive or OneDrive. For added security, encrypt files before uploading and share the encryption key separately.

Q2: Can video conferencing tools be hacked?
A: Yes, if not secured properly. Prevent unauthorized access by using passwords, waiting rooms, and encrypted platforms.

Q3: How do I identify a phishing email?
A: Look for red flags such as urgency, spelling errors, suspicious links, and unverified senders. When in doubt,

contact the sender directly through a verified channel.

Q4: Are free messaging apps safe for work communication?

A: While some free apps like Signal offer strong encryption, assess whether the app meets your organization's security policies and compliance requirements.

Q5: Should I use personal devices for work communication?

A: It's best to use company-provided devices with managed security settings. If personal devices must be used, ensure they are secured with encryption, antivirus software, and regular updates.

By adopting these measures, businesses and remote workers can significantly enhance the security of their communication and collaboration tools, safeguarding sensitive information and maintaining productivity in the digital workplace.

Chapter 5: Building a Secure Remote Work Culture

Building a secure remote work culture is essential for organizations to mitigate cybersecurity risks and ensure operational continuity. The shift to remote work has expanded the attack surface for cybercriminals, making employees a critical line of defense. By fostering a culture that prioritizes cybersecurity, businesses can reduce vulnerabilities, improve compliance, and create a workforce that actively contributes to securing company assets. This chapter explores the importance of employee education, the implementation of clear security policies, and the role of continuous training in cultivating a security-first mindset.

Educating Employees on Cybersecurity Best Practices

Employees are often the weakest link in an organization's security chain. Cyberattacks like phishing, ransomware, and social engineering frequently exploit human error rather than technical vulnerabilities. Educating employees is a fundamental step toward reducing these risks.

1. Highlighting the Importance of Cybersecurity

Many employees fail to recognize the critical role they play in maintaining organizational security. Begin by raising awareness about:

- The potential consequences of a security breach, such as financial losses, reputational damage, and legal penalties.

- How everyday actions, such as clicking on suspicious links or using weak passwords, can lead to significant security incidents.

2. Teaching Practical Cybersecurity Practices

Provide employees with actionable steps to secure their digital work environment:

- **Password Management:** Encourage the use of strong, unique passwords and password managers. Teach employees the importance of avoiding reused passwords.
- **Phishing Awareness:** Train employees to identify phishing emails by looking for red flags like grammatical errors, urgent requests, or suspicious links.
- **Safe Browsing Habits:** Educate employees on avoiding unverified

websites and downloading files from trusted sources only.

- **Device Security:** Stress the importance of locking devices when unattended and ensuring that software updates are installed promptly.

3. Using Real-Life Examples

Illustrate the impact of cybersecurity lapses through real-world case studies. For example:

- A phishing email that compromised an organization's sensitive data.
- A ransomware attack caused by an employee clicking on a malicious link.
  These examples make the risks tangible and emphasize the importance of vigilance.

Creating and Enforcing Clear Remote Work Security Policies

Policies provide a structured approach to managing cybersecurity risks. They set expectations, define acceptable behavior, and outline consequences for non-compliance.

1. Key Elements of a Remote Work Security Policy

A comprehensive remote work security policy should cover:

- **Device Usage:** Specify whether employees can use personal devices for work. If allowed, detail the security measures required (e.g., antivirus software, encryption).
- **Access Controls:** Define who can access specific resources and ensure that access is granted on a need-to-know basis.
- **Secure Communication:** Mandate the use of approved

communication tools and discourage the use of unsecured platforms for work-related discussions.

- **Data Protection:** Establish guidelines for handling, storing, and transmitting sensitive information.
- **Incident Reporting:** Provide clear instructions for reporting suspected security incidents, including whom to contact and the steps to take.

2. Ensuring Policy Compliance

A well-drafted policy is only effective if it is enforced. Strategies to ensure compliance include:

- **Regular Audits:** Periodically review compliance with security policies.
- **Monitoring Tools:** Implement tools to track policy adherence,

such as endpoint management systems.

- **Clear Consequences:** Outline disciplinary actions for policy violations, such as restricted access or formal warnings.

3. Supporting Employees

Policies should balance security requirements with employee productivity and convenience. Provide resources like IT support and access to secure tools to help employees comply with policies.

Conducting Regular Security Training and Awareness Programs

Security training should be an ongoing process that evolves alongside emerging threats. Regular training sessions keep employees informed and prepared to handle new challenges.

1. Designing Effective Training Programs

Effective training programs should:

- **Be Interactive:** Use simulations, quizzes, and role-playing to engage employees.
- **Address Specific Risks:** Tailor training content to address the unique risks associated with remote work.
- **Include All Employees:** Ensure training is mandatory for all team members, from entry-level employees to executives.

2. Using Phishing Simulations

Phishing simulations are a powerful tool to test and educate employees. These exercises involve sending simulated phishing emails to employees and tracking their responses. Use the results to identify vulnerabilities and provide targeted training.

3. Keeping Training Relevant

Cybersecurity threats are constantly evolving. Update training materials regularly to reflect new threats and best practices. For example:

- Include guidance on avoiding business email compromise (BEC) scams.
- Address risks associated with emerging technologies like IoT devices in home offices.

4. Building a Feedback Loop

Encourage employees to provide feedback on training programs. Use their insights to refine content and address areas where additional support is needed.

Cultivating a Security-First Mindset

A secure remote work culture extends beyond compliance; it requires employees to internalize cybersecurity as a shared responsibility. Foster this mindset by:

- **Recognizing Positive Behavior:** Reward employees who demonstrate strong security practices, such as reporting phishing attempts.
- **Leadership Involvement:** Ensure leaders model secure behaviors and emphasize the importance of cybersecurity in company communications.
- **Encouraging Open Communication:** Create an environment where employees feel comfortable reporting security concerns without fear of blame.

FAQs: Encouraging a Security-First Mindset

Q1: Why is employee education essential for cybersecurity?
A: Employees are often targeted by cybercriminals through phishing and social engineering attacks. Educating them reduces the risk of human error and strengthens overall security.

Q2: How often should security training be conducted?
A: Training should be conducted at least annually, with additional sessions whenever new threats or tools emerge. Regular refreshers help reinforce key concepts.

Q3: What should a remote work security policy include?
A: It should address device usage, access controls, secure communication, data protection, and incident reporting.

Clear expectations and guidelines are essential.

Q4: How can we ensure employees follow security policies?

A: Use a combination of regular audits, monitoring tools, and clear consequences for non-compliance. Providing IT support and secure tools also facilitates adherence.

Q5: How do phishing simulations improve security?

A: Phishing simulations test employees' ability to recognize phishing attempts and provide insights into areas where additional training is needed.

By educating employees, implementing robust policies, and fostering a culture of security awareness, organizations can effectively mitigate the risks associated with remote work. A security-first mindset ensures that every employee plays an active role in protecting company assets; creating a resilient and secure remote work environment.

Chapter 6: Cloud Security for Remote Teams

As remote work becomes the norm, cloud services have become indispensable tools for businesses. They enable seamless collaboration, data storage, and application access from anywhere in the world. However, the convenience of cloud computing comes with its own set of security challenges. To ensure that cloud environments remain secure, organizations must implement robust security measures that protect data, control access, and address emerging threats.

The Role of Cloud Services in Remote Work

Cloud services form the backbone of remote work infrastructure by offering scalable, on-demand access to resources. Key roles of cloud services include:

1. Enhancing Collaboration

Cloud platforms like Microsoft 365, Google Workspace, and Slack enable remote teams to collaborate in real-time, sharing documents, conducting virtual meetings, and managing projects seamlessly.

2. Streamlining Data Storage and Access

Cloud storage solutions such as Google Drive, OneDrive, and Dropbox allow employees to store and retrieve data without relying on physical devices. This ensures accessibility while reducing the risk of data loss due to device failure.

3. Supporting Business Continuity

Cloud services help maintain operational continuity during disruptions by providing remote access to critical systems and data. This is especially crucial during natural disasters, cyberattacks, or other emergencies.

4. Enabling Scalability

Organizations can scale their use of cloud resources based on demand, ensuring cost-efficiency. This flexibility is particularly beneficial for businesses with fluctuating workloads.

Securing Access to Cloud-Based Applications and Data

While cloud services offer numerous benefits, they also introduce security risks. Unauthorized access to cloud accounts or applications can result in data breaches, financial loss, and reputational damage. To mitigate these risks, organizations must focus on securing access to their cloud environments.

1. Implementing Strong Authentication Mechanisms

- Use **multi-factor authentication (MFA)** to add an extra layer of security to user accounts.
- Encourage employees to use strong, unique passwords and password managers to prevent credential reuse.
- Adopt single sign-on (SSO) solutions to simplify authentication while maintaining security.

2. Enforcing Role-Based Access Control (RBAC)

- Limit access to sensitive data and applications based on an employee's role.
- Regularly review and update permissions to ensure they align with current job responsibilities.

- Use the principle of least privilege to minimize the risk of accidental or intentional data exposure.

3. Monitoring User Activity

- Deploy tools to monitor and log user activity within cloud environments.
- Analyze logs for unusual behavior, such as login attempts from unknown locations or unauthorized data access.
- Set up alerts to notify administrators of potential security incidents.

Data Encryption and Secure Backups in the Cloud

Data stored in the cloud is vulnerable to unauthorized access, making encryption and backups critical components of a robust security strategy.

1. Encrypting Data at Rest and in Transit

- Use end-to-end encryption to protect data during transmission between users and cloud servers.
- Ensure that cloud providers encrypt data stored on their servers. Look for providers that comply with industry standards, such as AES-256 encryption.

2. Implementing Secure Backup Strategies

- Schedule regular backups of critical data to ensure it can be restored in the event of data loss or corruption.
- Store backups in geographically diverse locations to protect against regional disasters.

- Test backup and recovery procedures periodically to verify their effectiveness.

3. Verifying Provider Security

- Choose cloud providers that comply with established security frameworks, such as ISO 27001, SOC 2, or GDPR (if applicable).
- Review the provider's security policies, including their data retention and destruction practices.

Managing Permissions and Access Control

Managing permissions and access control effectively reduces the risk of unauthorized data access. Organizations must adopt a proactive approach to permissions management.

1. Centralized Identity and Access Management (IAM)

- Use IAM solutions to centralize user access across multiple cloud platforms.
- Implement policies to enforce strong authentication and password rotation.

2. Periodic Access Reviews

- Conduct regular audits of user access to ensure permissions align with business needs.
- Revoke access for employees who leave the organization or change roles.

3. Securing API Access

- If using cloud APIs, restrict access to authorized applications and developers.

- Rotate API keys periodically and monitor API usage for suspicious activity.

FAQs: Protecting Data in the Cloud

Q1: Why is multi-factor authentication (MFA) important for cloud security?
A: MFA adds an extra layer of security by requiring users to verify their identity through multiple factors, such as a password and a one-time code sent to their mobile device. This makes it significantly harder for attackers to gain unauthorized access.

Q2: How can encryption protect cloud data?

A: Encryption scrambles data into unreadable formats, ensuring that only authorized users with the correct decryption keys can access it. This protects sensitive information from being accessed by unauthorized parties, even if data is intercepted or stolen.

Q3: What is the principle of least privilege, and how does it apply to cloud security?

A: The principle of least privilege ensures that users are granted only the permissions necessary to perform their job functions. This minimizes the risk of accidental or malicious misuse of access rights.

Q4: How often should cloud access permissions be reviewed?

A: Access permissions should be reviewed quarterly or whenever there are significant changes in personnel, roles, or projects. Regular reviews help identify and remove unnecessary access rights.

Q5: How can organizations ensure their cloud provider is secure?

A: Organizations should select providers that comply with industry security standards, conduct regular audits, and provide transparent security policies. Additionally, reviewing the provider's service level agreements (SLAs) can clarify their responsibilities in maintaining data security.

By securing access, encrypting data, and managing permissions effectively, businesses can significantly enhance the security of their cloud environments. These measures not only protect sensitive data but also foster trust among employees, customers, and stakeholders. In today's remote work landscape, prioritizing cloud security is no longer optional—it is a critical component of operational success.

Chapter 7: Remote Work Incident Response and Recovery

Cybersecurity incidents are an unfortunate reality in today's interconnected world, and remote work setups are particularly vulnerable. Whether it's a phishing attack, malware infection, or data breach, the ability to respond swiftly and effectively is crucial to minimizing damage. This chapter focuses on recognizing incidents, responding to them, creating a robust incident response plan, and ensuring effective recovery.

Recognizing and Responding to a Security Breach

Timely recognition of a security breach is critical to mitigating its impact. Security breaches often exhibit warning signs, and understanding these indicators can empower remote teams to act promptly.

1. Common Indicators of a Security Breach

- **Unusual Login Activity:** Login attempts from unfamiliar devices, locations, or IP addresses.
- **System Anomalies:** Unexpected system behavior, such as slow performance, unauthorized software installations, or unexplainable file modifications.
- **Data Access Irregularities:** Large-scale data downloads or deletions.
- **Phishing Symptoms:** Multiple employees reporting suspicious emails or being redirected to fake login pages.
- **Alerts from Security Tools:** Notifications from antivirus software, firewalls, or endpoint detection tools.

2. Immediate Steps to Take

- **Disconnect from the Network:** Prevent further spread by isolating the affected system from the internet and internal networks.
- **Alert the IT or Security Team:** Notify your security team or managed service provider for immediate action.
- **Document Observations:** Record all suspicious activity and events leading to the breach to aid the investigation.
- **Avoid Tampering with Evidence:** Do not attempt to delete files or make changes that might interfere with forensic analysis.

Steps to Take During a Phishing or Malware Attack

Phishing and malware attacks are among the most common threats targeting remote workers. Knowing how to handle such incidents can reduce their impact.

1. Responding to Phishing Attacks

- **Report the Incident:** Use internal reporting mechanisms to alert the security team.
- **Do Not Click Links or Open Attachments:** Immediately stop interaction with the suspicious email or message.
- **Change Compromised Credentials:** If login details were submitted to a phishing site, update passwords for affected accounts immediately.
- **Monitor for Unusual Activity:** Check for unauthorized transactions or changes in accounts linked to the exposed credentials.

2. Handling Malware Infections

- **Run Antivirus Software:** Perform a full system scan using up-to-date antivirus or endpoint protection tools.
- **Quarantine Infected Devices:** Disconnect the infected system to prevent malware from spreading to other devices or networks.
- **Follow Incident Reporting Protocols:** Notify the IT team for further instructions and investigation.
- **Restore from Backup:** If files are corrupted or encrypted, retrieve them from a secure, recent backup.

Creating an Incident Response Plan for Remote Teams

A well-structured incident response plan (IRP) is essential for mitigating risks and ensuring that all team members know their roles during a cyber event.

1. Key Components of an Incident Response Plan

- **Defined Roles and Responsibilities:** Assign roles such as incident commander, communication lead, and forensic analyst.
- **Incident Categorization:** Establish criteria to classify incidents by severity (e.g., low, medium, high).
- **Clear Communication Channels:** Designate secure methods for reporting and communicating during an incident.
- **Step-by-Step Response Procedures:** Outline actions for common scenarios such as

phishing, ransomware, and insider threats.

- **Testing and Drills:** Conduct regular simulations to evaluate and improve the IRP's effectiveness.

2. Tailoring the Plan for Remote Teams

- **Provide Training:** Ensure remote workers understand the IRP and their responsibilities.
- **Use Collaboration Tools:** Leverage secure platforms for incident coordination and updates.
- **Account for Time Zones:** Adapt the plan to accommodate team members working across different time zones.
- **Secure Endpoint Access:** Ensure remote devices have tools for isolating threats, such as remote wipe and lock capabilities.

Post-Incident Recovery and Data Restoration

The recovery phase focuses on restoring normal operations, repairing systems, and learning from the incident to prevent future occurrences.

1. Steps for Recovery

- **Assess the Damage:** Determine the scope of the breach, including affected systems, data, and users.
- **Eliminate the Threat:** Remove malware, secure accounts, and patch vulnerabilities.
- **Restore Data:** Use verified backups to recover lost or corrupted data. Ensure backups are scanned for malware before restoration.
- **Reinforce Security Measures:** Update firewalls, antivirus

definitions, and endpoint security tools to address exploited vulnerabilities.

2. Learning from the Incident

- **Conduct a Post-Mortem Analysis:** Document the timeline, root cause, and impact of the incident.
- **Revise Security Policies:** Update remote work policies to address identified gaps.
- **Share Lessons Learned:** Communicate findings with employees and stakeholders to foster awareness.
- **Implement Monitoring Improvements:** Enhance logging and monitoring to detect future threats more effectively.

FAQs: Handling Cyber Incidents Effectively

Q1: What is the first step to take after detecting a potential breach?

A: The first step is to isolate the affected system by disconnecting it from the network. This prevents the threat from spreading and preserves evidence for investigation.

Q2: How can phishing attacks be identified?

A: Phishing emails often have suspicious sender addresses, urgent or threatening language, misspellings, and links leading to unfamiliar websites. Hover over links to check their legitimacy before clicking.

Q3: Why are backups crucial for recovery?

A: Backups ensure that you can restore critical data and systems after a breach or ransomware attack. They minimize downtime and reduce the impact of data loss.

Q4: How often should incident response plans be tested?

A: Incident response plans should be tested at least annually or whenever there are significant changes to the IT environment, staff, or threat landscape.

Q5: What are the benefits of conducting a post-incident analysis?

A: Post-incident analysis helps organizations understand what went wrong, identify weaknesses, and implement improvements to prevent similar incidents in the future.

Chapter 8: Essential Tools and Resources for Remote Work Security

Securing a remote work environment requires the right combination of tools and resources to protect sensitive data, devices, and communication channels. With cyber threats constantly evolving, businesses and remote workers must stay ahead by using advanced security solutions. This chapter explores essential tools, their roles in securing remote work, and how to choose the right ones for your setup.

Virtual Private Networks (VPNs): A Must-Have for Remote Workers

A Virtual Private Network (VPN) is a critical tool for remote work security, enabling employees to access company resources securely over the internet. It creates an encrypted "tunnel" for data, protecting it from interception by malicious actors.

1. Benefits of Using a VPN

- **Encryption:** VPNs encrypt internet traffic, making it unreadable to attackers.
- **Anonymity:** VPNs hide the user's IP address, enhancing privacy.
- **Secure Access:** VPNs provide safe connections to company servers and cloud-based tools.
- **Protection on Public Wi-Fi:** VPNs protect data when using potentially insecure networks, such as in cafes or airports.

2. Features to Look for in a VPN

- **Strong Encryption Protocols:** Look for VPNs that use protocols like OpenVPN or WireGuard.
- **No-Logs Policy:** Ensure the VPN provider does not store user activity logs.

- **Global Servers:** A wide network of servers improves speed and reliability.
- **Multi-Device Support:** Choose a VPN that supports all devices used for work.
- **Kill Switch:** This feature blocks internet access if the VPN connection drops, preventing accidental exposure.

3. Recommended VPN Services for Remote Work

- **NordVPN:** Known for its strong encryption, no-logs policy, and fast speeds.
- **ExpressVPN:** Offers top-notch security features and user-friendly apps.
- **ProtonVPN:** Focuses on privacy with robust encryption and transparency.

- **Cisco AnyConnect:** Ideal for enterprise remote work setups with advanced security options.

Password Managers for Securing Credentials

Weak or reused passwords are among the leading causes of data breaches. Password managers simplify the process of creating, storing, and managing strong, unique passwords for every account.

1. Benefits of Password Managers

- **Generate Strong Passwords:** Automatically create complex passwords that are hard to crack.
- **Secure Storage:** Store passwords in an encrypted vault accessible only with a master password.

- **Autofill Capabilities:** Quickly log in to accounts without manually entering credentials.
- **Cross-Device Synchronization:** Access passwords securely from any device.

2. Key Features to Look For

- **Encryption Standards:** AES-256 encryption ensures data security.
- **Two-Factor Authentication (2FA):** Adds an extra layer of protection.
- **Password Sharing:** Securely share passwords with colleagues when necessary.
- **Breach Alerts:** Notify users if stored credentials are part of a data breach.

3. Recommended Password Managers

- **LastPass:** Popular for its user-friendly interface and robust security features.
- **Dashlane:** Offers dark web monitoring and a built-in VPN.
- **1Password:** Excellent for team collaboration with advanced sharing features.
- **Bitwarden:** An open-source option that provides strong security at an affordable price.

Endpoint Protection Platforms for Businesses

With employees working from various locations, endpoint protection platforms (EPP) are vital for securing devices such as laptops, smartphones, and tablets against cyber threats.

1. What is Endpoint Protection?

EPP is a comprehensive security solution that protects endpoints from malware, ransomware, phishing attacks, and unauthorized access.

2. Key Features of Endpoint Protection Platforms

- **Antivirus and Antimalware:** Detects and removes malicious software.
- **Real-Time Monitoring:** Continuously monitors for suspicious activity.
- **Data Encryption:** Secures sensitive information stored on endpoints.
- **Device Management:** Enables IT teams to enforce security policies remotely.
- **Threat Intelligence:** Uses AI and machine learning to identify and respond to emerging threats.

3. Recommended Endpoint Protection Solutions

- **Microsoft Defender for Endpoint:** Offers advanced threat protection and seamless integration with Windows devices.
- **CrowdStrike Falcon:** A cloud-based solution that combines endpoint detection with AI-driven analytics.
- **Symantec Endpoint Security:** Provides robust protection for both small businesses and enterprises.
- **McAfee Total Protection:** Comprehensive security with features like VPN and identity theft protection.

Recommended Security Software and Hardware for Remote Setups

The combination of reliable software and hardware enhances the overall security of a remote work environment. Here are some must-have solutions:

1. Security Software

- **Firewalls:** Essential for blocking unauthorized access to networks. Tools like **pfSense** or **Sophos XG Firewall** are highly effective.
- **Antivirus Software:** Programs like **Norton 360, Kaspersky,** and **ESET NOD32** protect against malware and viruses.
- **Email Security:** Solutions such as **Proofpoint** or **Barracuda** prevent phishing and spam emails.
- **Backup Software:** Tools like **Acronis True Image** or **Veeam Backup** ensure data integrity by maintaining secure backups.

2. Security Hardware

- **Secure Routers:** Use routers with built-in firewalls and VPN support, such as **Netgear Nighthawk** or **Asus RT-AX88U**.
- **Hardware Security Keys:** Devices like **YubiKey** or **Google Titan Key** enhance MFA by requiring physical verification.
- **External Hard Drives:** Encryptable drives such as **Seagate Secure** or **Western Digital My Passport** provide secure data storage.

FAQs: Choosing the Right Tools

Q1: Why is a VPN necessary for remote work?
A: A VPN encrypts internet traffic, protecting sensitive data from being intercepted, especially when using

public Wi-Fi or accessing company resources remotely.

Q2: How can I ensure my passwords are secure?
A: Use a password manager to create and store unique, complex passwords. Enable two-factor authentication for an added layer of security.

Q3: What's the difference between antivirus and endpoint protection?
A: Antivirus software focuses on detecting and removing malware, while endpoint protection includes additional features like real-time monitoring, data encryption, and device management.

Q4: Are free security tools reliable?
A: Free tools can offer basic protection,

but they often lack advanced features, regular updates, and customer support. Investing in premium solutions is recommended for better security.

Q5: How often should I update my security tools?

A: Security tools should be updated as soon as new versions are available. Regular updates ensure protection against the latest threats.

By leveraging these tools and resources, businesses and remote workers can significantly reduce their risk of cyber threats and create a more secure remote work environment. Choosing the right combination of solutions tailored to specific needs ensures robust protection and peace of mind.

Chapter 9: The Future of Secure Remote Work

As remote work becomes an integral part of the modern workplace, the cybersecurity landscape continues to evolve to meet emerging challenges. A decentralized workforce introduces new vulnerabilities, but it also drives innovation in tools, practices, and policies designed to secure remote environments. This chapter explores the future of secure remote work, focusing on emerging cyber threats, the role of artificial intelligence (AI) and automation, and trends shaping cybersecurity in a remote-first world.

Emerging Cyber Threats in a Decentralized Workforce

The rise of remote work has created new opportunities for cybercriminals, requiring businesses to anticipate and address future threats proactively. Here are some key threats that will shape the future:

1. Advanced Phishing and Social Engineering Attacks

Cybercriminals are leveraging increasingly sophisticated methods to deceive remote workers into revealing sensitive information. These attacks may involve:

- **Deepfake Technology:** Using AI-generated voice or video to impersonate trusted individuals.
- **Contextual Phishing:** Crafting highly personalized emails based on employee behavior and publicly available data.

2. Ransomware Evolution

Ransomware attacks are becoming more targeted and destructive, with attackers employing double extortion tactics:

- Encrypting data and demanding payment.
- Threatening to release stolen data publicly if the ransom is not paid.

3. Insider Threats in Hybrid Work Models

With employees splitting time between home and office, insider threats may rise due to:

- Mismanagement of sensitive data.
- Accidental or intentional breaches caused by insufficient monitoring.

4. Supply Chain Attacks

Remote work often relies on third-party tools and services. Cybercriminals are targeting supply chains to infiltrate multiple organizations through:

- **Compromised Software Updates:** Embedding malware into legitimate software updates.

- **Third-Party Breaches:**
  Exploiting vulnerabilities in
  service providers.

5. IoT Device Vulnerabilities

The growing use of Internet of Things
(IoT) devices in home offices increases
risk due to:

- Weak default passwords.
- Lack of firmware updates and
  security patches.

**The Role of Artificial Intelligence and
Automation in Remote Security**

Artificial intelligence (AI) and
automation are transforming the way
organizations address cybersecurity
challenges in a remote work
environment. These technologies
provide proactive, efficient, and scalable
solutions.

1. AI-Driven Threat Detection and Response

AI-powered tools analyze vast amounts of data in real time to:

- Identify anomalies and potential threats.
- Predict and prevent attacks before they occur.
- Automate responses to neutralize threats quickly.

2. Behavioral Analytics

AI monitors user behavior to detect unusual activities, such as:

- Accessing files at odd hours.
- Logging in from unfamiliar locations.

Behavioral analytics help identify compromised accounts and insider threats.

3. Automated Patch Management

Automation ensures that software and systems receive timely updates, reducing vulnerabilities caused by outdated applications. Key features include:

- Automatically identifying and applying patches.
- Minimizing downtime during updates.

4.   Enhanced   Passwordless Authentication

AI enables advanced authentication methods, such as:

- **Biometric Verification:** Fingerprints, facial recognition, or voice authentication.
- **Continuous Authentication:** Monitoring user behavior throughout a session to verify identity.

5. Machine Learning for Threat Intelligence

Machine learning algorithms analyze historical attack patterns to:

- Predict emerging threats.
- Provide actionable insights for developing defense strategies.

Trends in Cybersecurity Tools and Practices for Remote Work

The future of secure remote work is shaped by innovations in tools and best practices designed to address the unique challenges of a distributed workforce.

1. Zero Trust Security Model

The Zero Trust model operates on the principle of "never trust, always verify." Key components include:

- **Micro-Segmentation:** Dividing networks into smaller, secure zones.

- **Granular Access Controls:**
  Allowing users access only to
  necessary resources.
- **Continuous Monitoring:**
  Regularly verifying user identities
  and activities.

2. Secure Access Service Edge (SASE)

SASE integrates network security
functions with cloud-based services to
provide secure access regardless of
location. Features include:

- **Cloud Firewall:** Protects remote
  users accessing cloud applications.
- **Secure Web Gateway:** Blocks
  malicious websites and
  downloads.
- **Zero Trust Network Access
  (ZTNA):** Restricts access to
  specific applications.

3. Multi-Factor Authentication (MFA)
Evolution

Future MFA solutions will incorporate:

- Biometric and AI-based authentication.
- Context-aware authentication that considers location, device, and behavior.

4. Decentralized Identity Management

Blockchain technology is being explored for secure identity management, allowing users to control their digital identities without relying on centralized databases.

5. Cybersecurity as a Service (CaaS)

Organizations are outsourcing cybersecurity functions to specialized providers who offer:

- Advanced threat monitoring.
- Incident response services.
- Tailored security solutions for remote teams.

FAQs: Preparing for the Future of Remote Work Security

Q1: What are the biggest cybersecurity risks for remote work in the future?

A: Key risks include sophisticated phishing attacks, ransomware, insider threats, supply chain vulnerabilities, and IoT security gaps.

Q2: How can AI help secure remote work environments?

A: AI enhances security by detecting threats in real time, analyzing user behavior for anomalies, automating responses, and managing patches efficiently.

Q3: What is the Zero Trust Security Model, and why is it important?

A: The Zero Trust model assumes that no user or device is trusted by default. It requires strict identity verification and continuous monitoring, making it crucial for securing remote and hybrid work environments.

Q4: How will authentication methods evolve in the future?

A: Authentication will move towards passwordless solutions, using biometrics, AI, and context-aware techniques to enhance security and user experience.

Q5: What steps can businesses take to prepare for future cyber threats?

A: Businesses should:

- Adopt AI and automation for threat detection.
- Implement Zero Trust and SASE models.
- Regularly train employees on emerging threats.
- Invest in advanced cybersecurity tools and services.

The future of secure remote work lies in proactive measures, cutting-edge technology, and a strong culture of cybersecurity awareness. By staying ahead of emerging threats and embracing innovative solutions, businesses can create resilient remote work environments that safeguard their data, employees, and reputation.

Conclusion

As businesses increasingly embrace remote work, securing a decentralized workforce has become a critical priority. This book has explored the multi-faceted nature of remote work security, offering insights into the challenges, tools, and practices necessary to build a resilient and secure remote work environment. In this concluding chapter, we summarize the key takeaways and provide final thoughts on fostering a culture of cybersecurity that empowers both businesses and employees.

Key Takeaways from the Book

Securing remote work is not a one-time effort but a continuous process that involves technological innovation, robust policies, and employee engagement. The key takeaways from this book include:

1. Cybersecurity is a Shared Responsibility

Every stakeholder—employers, employees, and third-party vendors—plays a crucial role in maintaining a secure remote work environment. It is vital to:

- Educate employees on cybersecurity best practices.
- Ensure vendors adhere to strict security standards.
- Encourage a security-first mindset across all levels of the organization.

2. Threats to Remote Work are Evolving

The remote work landscape introduces unique threats, including phishing attacks, ransomware, and insider risks. Businesses must stay vigilant by:

- Continuously monitoring and assessing vulnerabilities.

- Investing in advanced threat detection tools.
- Regularly updating their cybersecurity frameworks to address emerging risks.

3. Technology is a Key Enabler

The right tools and technologies can significantly enhance remote work security. Essential solutions discussed include:

- Virtual Private Networks (VPNs) for secure connections.
- Multi-Factor Authentication (MFA) to prevent unauthorized access.
- Endpoint protection platforms to secure devices used in remote work.

4. Policies and Training are Fundamental

Technology alone is insufficient without clear policies and regular employee training. Organizations must:

- Develop comprehensive remote work security policies.
- Conduct regular security awareness programs.
- Provide employees with resources to identify and respond to cyber threats effectively.

5. The Future of Remote Work Requires Adaptability

As cyber threats evolve, so must security practices. Businesses should prepare for future challenges by:

- Embracing the Zero Trust Security model.
- Leveraging artificial intelligence (AI) and automation.
- Staying informed about cybersecurity trends and advancements.

Final Thoughts on Building a Resilient and Secure Remote Workforce

Remote work is here to stay, and with it comes a responsibility to ensure that employees and businesses thrive in a secure digital environment. Achieving this requires a holistic approach that combines technology, policies, and culture.

Fostering a Culture of Cybersecurity

The foundation of a secure remote workforce is a strong cybersecurity culture. This involves:

- Making security a part of daily work routines.
- Encouraging employees to report suspicious activities without fear of repercussions.
- Recognizing and rewarding proactive security practices.

Investing in the Future

Securing remote work is not just about addressing current challenges but also about anticipating future needs. Businesses that prioritize innovation, adaptability, and employee education will not only safeguard their operations but also gain a competitive edge in the digital economy.

Empowering Employees

Employees are the first line of defense against cyber threats. Empowering them with the knowledge, tools, and confidence to make secure decisions is one of the most effective ways to protect an organization. A secure remote work environment starts with informed and engaged employees.

Collaboration is Key

Building a resilient remote workforce requires collaboration between IT teams, business leaders, and employees.

Open communication and shared accountability foster an environment where security is a collective effort.

Looking Ahead

The transition to remote work has redefined how businesses operate, presenting both challenges and opportunities. While the cybersecurity landscape continues to evolve, the principles and strategies outlined in this book serve as a roadmap for businesses aiming to navigate this complex terrain effectively.

By prioritizing security, fostering collaboration, and embracing innovation, businesses can create resilient remote workforces that not only adapt to change but thrive in an increasingly digital world.

As you apply the concepts shared in this book, remember that cybersecurity is a journey, not a destination. Continuous learning, vigilance, and adaptability will ensure that your organization remains secure, agile, and prepared for whatever the future holds.

Appendices

The appendices serve as a practical reference section, providing tools, templates, and resources to reinforce the cybersecurity strategies discussed in the book. These appendices are designed to offer hands-on guidance to remote workers, IT administrators, and business leaders alike. Each appendix contains actionable content to help readers implement robust security measures tailored to their specific needs.

Appendix A: Cybersecurity Checklist for Remote Workers

A cybersecurity checklist is essential for ensuring that remote workers follow best practices and maintain a secure work environment. Below is a comprehensive checklist to guide employees in safeguarding their devices, networks, and data:

Device Security

1. Ensure all devices (laptops, smartphones, tablets) have up-to-date operating systems and software.
2. Install and regularly update antivirus and anti-malware software.
3. Enable device encryption to protect sensitive data.
4. Set strong, unique passwords for all accounts and devices.
5. Use Multi-Factor Authentication (MFA) wherever possible.

Network Security

6. Configure your home Wi-Fi network with WPA3 encryption.
7. Change default router passwords and regularly update them.
8. Avoid using public Wi-Fi for work; if necessary, use a Virtual Private Network (VPN).

9. Ensure your firewall is enabled and properly configured.

Work Practices

10. Log out of work applications and devices when not in use.
11. Avoid downloading unauthorized or suspicious files.
12. Regularly back up important work data to a secure location.
13. Report any suspicious activity or potential breaches immediately.

Collaboration Tools

14. Use only authorized and secure communication platforms.
15. Verify file-sharing links before opening them.
16. Enable end-to-end encryption for messaging and video calls.

This checklist should be distributed to all remote workers as part of their onboarding and periodically updated to reflect emerging cybersecurity threats.

Below is a template for creating a robust remote work security policy tailored to an organization's needs:

[Company Name] Remote Work Security Policy

Purpose

This policy outlines the security requirements for remote work to protect company data, devices, and systems from unauthorized access, theft, or damage.

Scope

This policy applies to all employees, contractors, and third-party vendors who access company resources remotely.

Key Requirements

1. **Device Security**

   o Employees must use company-issued devices or obtain explicit approval to use personal devices.
   o Devices must have updated antivirus software and encryption enabled.

2. **Network Security**

   o Remote work must be conducted on a secure Wi-Fi network with strong encryption.
   o Employees must connect to the company VPN when accessing internal systems.

3. **Access Control**

   o Strong passwords must be used for all work accounts.
   o Multi-Factor Authentication (MFA) is required for accessing sensitive data.

4. **Data Protection**

   - Confidential information must not be stored on personal devices or shared via unauthorized platforms.
   - Data must be backed up regularly to approved storage locations.

5. **Incident Reporting**

   - Employees must report potential security incidents immediately to the IT department.

Compliance

Failure to comply with this policy may result in disciplinary action, up to and including termination.

Acknowledgment

By signing below, I acknowledge that I have read, understood, and agree to abide by this policy.

Employee   Name:

_____

Signature:

_____

Date: _____

Appendix C: Incident Response Plan Template for Remote Teams

A structured incident response plan is critical for managing cybersecurity breaches effectively. Below is a template to help businesses develop their own plans:

[Company Name] Incident Response Plan

Objective

To provide a framework for identifying, managing, and recovering from cybersecurity incidents in a remote work environment.

Incident Response Steps

1. **Identification**

   - Monitor systems for signs of potential breaches (e.g., unusual login attempts, unauthorized access).
   - Encourage employees to report suspicious activities immediately.

2. **Containment**

   - Disconnect compromised devices from the network.
   - Restrict access to affected accounts or systems.

3. **Eradication**

   - Remove malware or unauthorized software.
   - Reset passwords and review access permissions.

4. **Recovery**

- Restore data from secure backups.
- Re-enable access after verifying system integrity.

5. **Post-Incident Analysis**

- Conduct a detailed review to identify vulnerabilities.
- Update security policies and tools to prevent future incidents.

Roles and Responsibilities

- **IT Team:** Lead incident response efforts.
- **Employees:** Report incidents and follow security protocols.
- **Management:** Approve resources and communicate with stakeholders.

Contact Information

- IT Support: [Email/Phone Number]

- Incident Reporting: [Link/Email Address]

Appendix D: List of Recommended Cybersecurity Tools

The following tools are highly recommended for enhancing remote work security across devices, networks, and cloud services:

1. Virtual Private Networks (VPNs)

- **NordVPN:** Robust encryption and fast speeds.
- **ExpressVPN:** Reliable and user-friendly.
- **Cisco AnyConnect:** Enterprise-grade VPN solution.

2. Password Managers

- **LastPass:** Secure password storage with sharing features.
- **1Password:** Excellent for families and teams.

- **Dashlane:** Includes a dark web monitoring tool.

3. Endpoint Protection Platforms

- **CrowdStrike Falcon:** Advanced endpoint detection and response (EDR).
- **Symantec Endpoint Security:** Comprehensive antivirus and firewall protection.
- **Microsoft Defender for Endpoint:** Integrated with Microsoft 365 for seamless security.

4. Communication Tools with Built-In Security

- **Zoom with Encryption:** Secure video conferencing.
- **Microsoft Teams:** Secure collaboration with compliance options.
- **Slack Enterprise Grid:** Scalable and secure team communication.

5. Backup Solutions

- **Acronis Cyber Protect:**
  Combines backup with
  anti-malware.
- **Backblaze:** Affordable and
  user-friendly cloud backup.
- **Carbonite:** Ideal for small
  businesses.

This appendix provides a curated list of
tools to guide businesses and remote
workers in making informed decisions
about their cybersecurity investments.

These appendices are intended to be
living documents, updated regularly to
address the evolving cybersecurity
landscape and to incorporate new tools,
technologies, and practices. By
leveraging these resources,
organizations and individuals can fortify
their defenses and confidently navigate
the challenges of remote work security.

www.ingramcontent.com/pod-product-compliance
Lightning Source LLC
LaVergne TN
LVHW051653050326
832903LV00032B/3786